My Kitten

A Record Book of Memories & More

PLACE PHOTO HERE

My Kitten

A Record Book of Memories & More

Printed in the United States of America
by G&R Publishing Co.

Distributed By:

507 Industrial Street
Waverly, IA 50677

ISBN 13: 978-1-56383-234-5
ISBN 10: 1-56383-234-8
Item #9621

This Book Belongs To:

_____

All About Me

All About Me

Birth Date: _____

Breed: _____

Color: _____

Date I was purchased or adopted: _____

I was purchased or adopted from: _____

_____

_____
My Grandfather

_____
My Father

_____
My Grandmother

_____
Me

_____
My Grandfather

_____
My Mother

_____
My Grandmother

My First Photo

PLACE PHOTO HERE

My Name is

My full name is: _____

This is how my owner chose my name: _____

_____

_____

My name means: _____

_____

_____

Other names my owner liked were: _____

_____

My nicknames are: _____

_____

About My Breed of Cat

My breed is: _____

The different colors for cats in my breed are: _____

When I'm full grown I could be this tall: _____

And I could weigh this much: _____

The origin of my breed is: _____

_____

_____

My breed is known for: _____

_____

_____

Some interesting things about my breed: _____

_____

What's Unique About Me

As a kitten...

My hair color is: _____

My eyes are: _____

I weigh: _____

My nose is: _____

My paws are: _____

My ears are: _____

My personality is: _____

_____

Other special things about me: _____

_____

_____

My Paw Prints

Vet Visits

My veterinarian is: _____

Date   Reason for visit

_____   _____

_____   _____

_____   _____

_____   _____

_____   _____

_____   _____

_____   _____

_____   _____

Vaccinations, etc.
Vaccinations, Worming, & Flea Treatments

Date   For

_____   _____

_____   _____

_____   _____

_____   _____

_____   _____

_____   _____

_____   _____

_____   _____

Growth Chart

Growth Chart

Date	Height	Weight

My New Family

My New Family

The _____ Family

This is where we live:

_____

_____

My family members & other pets:

_____

_____

_____

_____

_____

_____

PLACE PHOTO HERE

10

Me & My Family

My First Day Home

My First Day Home

Date _____

This is what I did: _____

_____

_____

_____

This is what I saw: _____

_____

_____

_____

PLACE PHOTO HERE

My Typical Day

My Typical Day

12:00 a.m.	_____	12:00 p.m.	_____
1:00 a.m.	_____	1:00 p.m.	_____
2:00 a.m.	_____	2:00 p.m.	_____
3:00 a.m.	_____	3:00 p.m.	_____
4:00 a.m.	_____	4:00 p.m.	_____
5:00 a.m.	_____	5:00 p.m.	_____
6:00 a.m.	_____	6:00 p.m.	_____
7:00 a.m.	_____	7:00 p.m.	_____
8:00 a.m.	_____	8:00 p.m.	_____
9:00 a.m.	_____	9:00 p.m.	_____
10:00 a.m.	_____	10:00 p.m.	_____
11:00 a.m.	_____	11:00 p.m.	_____

My First Bath

My First Bath

Date: _____

Where: _____

_____

My reaction: _____

_____

_____

_____

_____

_____

_____

PLACE PHOTO HERE

14

My First Roadtrip

My First Roadtrip

PLACE PHOTO HERE

Date: _____

I traveled to: _____

Number of miles: _____

My reaction: _____

_____

_____

_____

_____

_____

15

My First Birthday

My First Birthday

Date: _____

I celebrated by: _____

_____

_____

_____

_____

I received: _____

_____

_____

_____

PLACE PHOTO HERE

16

My First Holiday

PLACE PHOTO HERE

Date: _____

Holiday: _____

To celebrate, I: _____

_____

_____

_____

_____

Comments: _____

_____

_____

 # Cat Fights

Date: _____

Where: _____

I got in a fight with: _____

_____

_____

My reaction: _____

_____

_____

_____

PLACE PHOTO HERE

Climbing Around

Climbing Around

PLACE PHOTO HERE

Date: _____

Where: _____

This is what I climbed: _____

_____

Comments: _____

_____

_____

_____

_____

_____

Me and Mischief
The Day I Got Into Mischief

Date: _____

This is what I did: _____

_____

_____

_____

_____

My owner's reaction: _____

_____

_____

_____

PLACE PHOTO HERE

Me and Mischief
The Day I Got Into Mischief

PLACE PHOTO HERE

Date: _____

This is what I did: _____

_____

_____

_____

_____

My owner's reaction: _____

_____

_____

_____

_____

21

My Favorite Things

My Favorite Things

Toy _____

Treat _____

Item to chew _____

Place to sleep _____

Place to claw _____

Game to play _____

Place to play _____

Place to climb _____

Thing to chase _____

Place to eat _____

Thing to rub against _____

My Favorite Things

My Favorite Things

PLACE PHOTO HERE

Tricks & Training

		Comments	Date
☐	Litter trained	_____	_____
☐	Learned my name	_____	_____
☐	Caught mice	_____	_____
☐	Came when called	_____	_____
☐	Chased string	_____	_____
☐		_____	_____
☐		_____	_____
☐		_____	_____
☐		_____	_____
☐		_____	_____
☐		_____	_____

Tricks & Training Snapshots

Tricks & Training Snapshots

My Favorite Season is...

My Favorite Season is...

_____

PLACE PHOTO HERE

because... _____

_____

_____

26

My Least Favorite Season is...

My Least Favorite Season is...

PLACE PHOTO HERE

because... _____

_____

_____

My Best Friend

Name: _____

We have fun when we: _____

_____

_____

_____

_____

Our favorite memories: _____

_____

_____

_____

PLACE PHOTO HERE

My Pet Friends

My Pet Friends

PLACE PHOTO HERE

Name

His or her owner is

_____

_____

_____

_____

_____

_____

All Dressed Up

Date: _____

Occasion: _____

_____

My reaction: _____

_____

_____

_____

_____

_____

PLACE PHOTO HERE

My Brag Page

My Brag Page

PLACE PHOTO HERE

Date:_____

This is what I did: _____

_____

_____

_____

_____

_____

_____

_____

_____

What Makes Me Meow

Comments

- ☐ Dogs _____
- ☐ Strangers _____
- ☐ Mailman _____
- ☐ Cars _____
- ☐ TV _____
- ☐ When I'm hungry _____
- ☐ _____
- ☐ _____
- ☐ _____
- ☐ _____
- ☐ _____

What Makes Me Purr

What Makes Me Purr

Comments

☐ People _____

☐ Attention _____

☐ Being petted _____

☐ Sleeping _____

☐ Being scratched _____

☐ _____

☐ _____

☐ _____

☐ _____

☐ _____

☐ _____

I've Been an Angel

I've Been an Angel

Date: _____

This is what I did: _____

_____

_____

_____

_____

My owner's reaction: _____

_____

_____

_____

_____

PLACE PHOTO HERE

Meal Time

Meal Time

PLACE PHOTO HERE

My favorite cat food is:_____

_____

_____

My favorite catnip is:_____

_____

_____

My favorite treats are:_____

_____

_____

My favorite way to eat is:_____

_____

_____

Recipes

Feline Fishballs

1 (8 oz.) can tuna in oil, drained

2 oz. cooked herring, skin removed

3 baby carrots, boiled and mashed

1 egg, beaten

3 Tbls. shredded cheese

2 Tbls. whole grain bread crumbs or rolled oats

2 Tbls. tomato paste

2 tsp. brewer's yeast*

¼ tsp. catnip

In medium bowl, combine all ingredients and mix well. Roll dough into 1" balls and place rounds 1" apart on greased baking sheets. Bake at 350° for 15 to 20 minutes, or until golden brown and firm. Allow to cool on wire racks before storing in a covered container in refrigerator.

*Note: Store in refrigerator up to 3 weeks or in freezer up to 1 year. *Brewer's yeast is an excellent source of essential fatty acids and B-Complex vitamins, helping give your kitty a glossy coat and stable nervous system. It has also been known to prevent flea infestation.*

Yummy Treats for Me

Recipes

Holy Mackerel Kitty Snacks

½ cup canned mackerel, drained and crumbled

1 cup whole grain bread crumbs

1 Tbls. vegetable oil or bacon grease

1 egg, beaten

½ tsp. brewer's yeast, optional*

In a medium bowl, combine all ingredients and mix well. Drop dough by ¼ teaspoonfuls 1" apart onto a greased baking sheet. Bake at 350° for 8 minutes. Remove from oven and let snacks cool completely on wire racks before storing in a covered container in refrigerator.

*Note: Store in refrigerator up to 3 weeks or in freezer for up to 1 year. *Brewer's yeast is an excellent source of essential fatty acids and B-Complex vitamins, helping give your kitty a glossy coat and stable nervous system. It has also been known to prevent flea infestation.*

Yummy Treats for Me

Kitty Tuna Treats

1 cup whole wheat flour

6 oz. can tuna in oil, undrained

1 Tbls. vegetable oil or bacon grease

1 egg, beaten

In a medium bowl, combine all ingredients and mix well. If mixture is too thick, add small amounts of water until a soft dough forms. Turn dough onto a lightly floured surface and roll out to ¼" thickness. Cut shapes out of dough with a cookie cutter and place 1" apart on an ungreased baking sheet. Bake at 350° for 20 minutes, or until treats are firm. Remove from oven and let cool completely on wire racks.

Note: Store in refrigerator up to 3 weeks or in freezer for up to 1 year.

When I'm Happy

When I'm Happy

PLACE PHOTO HERE

These things make me happy: _____

_____

_____

_____

_____

My tail: _____

_____

My meow or purr is: _____

_____

I also: _____

_____

_____

When I'm Sad

When I'm Sad

These things make me sad: _____

_____

_____

_____

_____

My tail: _____

_____

My meow or purr is: _____

_____

I also: _____

_____

_____

PLACE PHOTO HERE

When I'm Grumpy

When I'm Grumpy

PLACE PHOTO HERE

These things make me grumpy: _____

_____

_____

_____

_____

My tail: _____

_____

My meow or purr is: _____

_____

I also: _____

_____

_____

When I'm Scared

When I'm Scared

These things make me scared: _____

_____

_____

_____

_____

My tail: _____

_____

My meow or purr is: _____

_____

I also: _____

_____

PLACE PHOTO HERE

42

Things I Like to Pounce

Things I Like to Pounce

- ☐ Mice _____
- ☐ Pillow _____
- ☐ Birds _____
- ☐ Balls and toys _____
- ☐ _____
- ☐ _____
- ☐ _____
- ☐ _____
- ☐ _____
- ☐ _____
- ☐ _____

Favorite Activities

PLACE PHOTO HERE

_____

_____

_____

My Bad Habits

My Bad Habits

PLACE PHOTO HERE

Bad Habits: _____

_____

_____

_____

_____

_____

My owner's reaction: _____

_____

_____

_____

_____

_____

45

Naptime

Playtime

PLACE PHOTO HERE

Special Moments

Special Moments

PLACE PHOTO HERE

Special Moments

Special Moments

PLACE PHOTO HERE

The Funny Things I Do

The Funny Things I Do

I'm funny when: _____

_____

_____

_____

_____

_____

My owner's reaction: _____

_____

_____

_____

_____

PLACE PHOTO HERE

Journaling

Favorite Photo

Journaling

Journaling

Snapshots

Journaling

Journaling

Caught on Camera

While My Owner Was Gone

While My Owner Was Gone, I Stayed With

Dates: _____

Who watched me: _____

Reaction: _____

I acted: _____

_____

Dates: _____

Who watched me: _____

Reaction: _____

I acted: _____

_____

Dates: _____

Who watched me: _____

Reaction: _____

I acted: _____

_____

Dates: _____

Who watched me: _____

Reaction: _____

I acted: _____

_____

Important Contacts

Name: _____

Title: _____

Address: _____

_____

Phone Number: _____

Name: _____

Title: _____

Address: _____

_____

Phone Number: _____

Name: _____

Title: _____

Address: _____

_____

Phone Number: _____

Name: _____

Title: _____

Address: _____

_____

Phone Number: _____

Resources

Resources

Kitty food: _____

Available at: _____

_____

Kitty supplies: _____

Available at: _____

_____

Other: _____

Available at: _____

_____

Other: _____

Available at: _____

_____

Books, Websites and Other resources:

_____

_____

_____

_____

_____

_____

_____

_____

_____

PLACE PHOTO HERE